Emotion

and

Venom

Rene Xaviere

Haiku 01

Black, rat-stalking cat
Skulking in shadows, waiting
For whiskered prey.

Haiku 2

Wasted, drug-addled
Worms squirming in my brain;
Such is poetry.

Haiku 03

Thorazine smiles:
Wretched white zombies dreaming
Halidol-laced dreams.

Haiku 04

Suicide watch nurse:
Demonic eyeballs record
Eternal slumber.

Haiku 05

Lone gray wolf lurking,
Dark insidious dreamscapes
Unfurling the night.

Haiku 06

Red lightning crashes,
Psychoschizophrenic rage
Cumulates in death.

Burnt Offerings

Burning hot embers
Of yesterday's tomorrow
Are today's ashes.

Haiku 07

Books, movies, TV
Slander and plagiarism,
Oh, what wicked fun.

Red

Crimson petals bloom
In wonder, torn asunder
Scarlet scars remain.

Heat

After-images
Of erotic horror shows
Burning in my mind.

Haiku 08

Wood hung savior,
Crucifixion addiction:
Crosses everywhere.

Haiku 09

Magnolia leaves,
Wet wind-blown, driving rain torn,
Scuttleling like rats.

Haiku 10

Passion-filled fury:
The siren song of the damned
Echoes death's chambers.

Haiku 11

Opium poppy,
A flower in a wasteland;
Nuclear winter.

Haiku 12

Snakes, lizards, spiders
Slither, creep, crawl silently
Towards sleeping child.

Haiku 13

In sacred forest
Unholy spectres rising;
Whispers of the past.

Haiku 14

Divine tragedy:
Fixed and dilated look
In violet-blue eyes.

Haiku 15

A torrent of smoke,
The voracious inferno
Devours them all.

Allure

Sublime temptation,
Wicked devices and lies
Enrapture the heart.

Haiku 16

Bloodless, lifeless shell
My black and blue Valentine,
Time to say goodbye.

Haiku 17

Razor blade apples,
Cyanide-laced chocolate
Mark childhood's end.

Haiku 18

God-like darkness falls

Upon unsuspecting fools

Led to the slaughter.

Haiku 19

Roaring in torment,

Banshees of wind cycling up;

Goblin cries shrieking.

Haiku 20

Unbridled fury,

A herd of nightmare horses

Gallop from Hell's gate.

Haiku 21

Selfish, self-absorbed
Narcissistic psychopath:
Hidden other self.

Haiku 22

Buck knives and switchblades,
A sadistic puppeteer;
Rivers of blood flow.

Haiku 23

Self-immolating
Desperation rages on:
Sweet fires of Hell.

Into the blood

Subterranean

Ceremonial chamber;

Crimson immersion.

Haiku 24

Switchblade serenade,

Unleashed passion made fury

Cuts deep to the core.

Haiku 25

Nightfall approaching,

Interlopers encroaching;

Nothing left sacred.

Haiku 26

Guerilla warfare:
Ravages of shattered flesh,
Uzi suicide.

Haiku 27

Crazy hot anger,
A tumult of rage and grief:
Emotional catharsis.

Haiku 28

Silver desert sky,
Rattle of a diamondback;
Lightning strike snake bite.

Haiku 29

Chemical cocktail;

Medicate to educate

Empty-headed sheep.

Haiku 30

Death in a black robe

With melodramatic hood;

Scythe shines in moonlight.

Haiku 31

Chloform soaked rag,

Blood-splattered autopsy saw

With cranial blades.

Haiku 32

Burned-out white trash mind,

Jesus-loving hate mongers:

Midwest Dark Ages.

Haiku 33

Dark eyes with red tint,

Hideous ferocity

Screaming for vengeance.

Haiku 34

Fire and brimstone,

A twisted incarnation;

Satan's own design.

Brandy

Malice incarnate,

A worthless rancid dope-whore;

Modern day vampire.

Haiku 35

Beauty and fire,

A phantasm of petals

Cherry blossom pink.

Haiku 36

Aristocratic

Mechanical animals;

Society's pets.

Haiku 37

Enveloped by night,
This blessed sweet surrender
Broken by dawn's light.

Haiku 38

Blood, death, and horror,
Utopian ideas
Lead to destruction.

Haiku 39

Agony and rage,
Murder and brutality:
Eternal monster.

Haiku 40

Hard obligation,
Suggestion of destiny;
A fate determined.

Haiku 41

Archangel Michael
Celestial warrior
God's mercenary

Haiku 42

Blood, freedom, hunt, kill,
Melody of savagery;
Turmoil grows within.

Haiku 43

Voodoo moon whispers,

Wild wind caresses the night;

Nocturnal magic.

Haiku 44

Enveloped by night,

Cocooned in darkness:

Nocturnal chrysalis.

Haiku 45

From cradle to grave,

Death chases life since first breath;

All are born to die.

Haiku 46

Arcane energy,

Tainted, lust-filled requiem;

Death everlasting.

Haiku 47

Beggar's day Sunday,

A reviled revival

Placates the masses.

Roar

Thrilling confidence,

Animal ferocity

Radiates power.

Night wolf

Supernatural
Untamed midnight animal:
Maverick lupine.

Rapture

Oceans red with blood,
Cities of rotting corpses;
Apocalypse now.

Requiem

Sanctum Sanctorum,
Primitive arcane machines;
A vault of secrets.

Mantis

The praying mantis:

A ferocious carnivore,

With divine posture.

Haiku 48

Cathedral spires,

Steeple-shattering lightning,

Violent thunder.

Haiku 49

Rock crystal fragments,

A rain-shattered chandelier;

Extinguished beauty.

Haiku 50

Rage shudders the air,
Stark white bones of lightning crack
Across black-skinned sky.

Tempest

A sea of sorrow
Increases and falls again
In a storm of rage.

Haiku 51

Vapory darkness,
Palm trees thrashing in the night;
Iron realm of dreams.

Haiku 52

Burden of my heart
Weighs like a stone in my chest
Heavy with the past.

Haiku 53

Extinguished candles;
The portal out of darkness
Is revelation.

Haiku 54

Cold blue reflections,
Lightning flutters like dream fire
Across painted floor.

Haiku 55

Enduring freedom

Ignites primal ambition

In cold-blooded minds.

Haiku 56

Lemonade vodka,

A dirty little snicker;

Sexualized violence.

Drowning

Swimming in the dark,

Undertow in black water;

Oblivion looms.

Haiku 57

Red sky in the east,
Diamond fire horizon,
Sapphire, the west.

Haiku 58

Birthday cake icing,
Pink and white and sticky sweet
Smeared on blood-stained hands.

Haiku 59

A spiky shadow,
Busy spider spins a web
Between ceiling joists.

Inferno

Orange mask of flames,

Dragon fire tornado

Spreads across the streets.

Haiku 60

Symbolic killings,

Homicidal impulses,

Infect the spirit.

Nature

Crickets in the grass,

Moth wings tapping on windows:

A subtle chorus.

Haiku 61

Shadows are rising,
An amber-purple sunset;
Night blooming flowers.

Haiku 62

Twilight fading fast,
A shadow zombie army
Rising from the night.

Haiku 63

Deserted graveyard,
Modern day necropolis;
The silence of death.

Haiku 64

Copper scent of blood,
Thick sticky petals blooming
In crimson flowers.

Haiku 65

Suspended castles,
Vapor thin mirages hang
On thick walls of air.

Celestial

Flood of bloody light,
Reflected solar fire;
Chariots of flame.

Hollow power

Bore like a cannon,
.357 magnum;
Voice of a dragon.

Haiku 66

Animated corpse,
Rotted burial garments,
Carnival funhouse.

Haiku 67

Vermillion rose:
Ugly red flower of blood
Blossoms in the rain.

Haiku 68

Serpentine anger,
Tires hiss on wet pavement
For each passing car.

Apocalypse now

Doomsday explosion,
Waves of super-heated air
Vaporize the rain.

Haiku 69

Spectral energies
Radiating from the saints,
And souls of the dead.

Haiku 70

Bats flick through my head,
Bats with dark razor-edged wings
That cut like fire.

Haiku 71

Scurrying spiders
In the hollows of my bones
Weaving webs of ice.

Haiku 72

Showers of embers
From a celestial blaze
Look like falling rain.

Haiku 73

Feathery shadows,
Dangerous and menacing,
Talking to themselves.

Haiku 74

October twilight:
That intense crimson essence
Of burnt-out black sky.

Haiku 75

Night wind slowly blows,
Flutes across a rain gutter;
A low, mournful note.

Rising

Ascending full moon,

The conflict rages within

A nascent werewolf.

Haiku 76

Copper scent of blood,

Inescapable perfume

Ignites the senses.

Haiku 77

Lone strange bird of prey

Circling throughout the night,

Hunting on storm winds.

Haiku 78

Inky clouds spreading,
Black as the moonless night sky,
Throughout a jade sea.

Haiku 79

A cold metal blade,
In the velvety darkness,
Glints silver fire.

Haiku 80

Unmelodious
Symphony of destruction
Ringing in my ears.

Haiku 81

Ravenous jackals,
An overbearing power
Chewing on my mind.

Haiku 82

Bittersweet flower:
Muscle, fire, energy...
A weird night orchid.

Haiku 83

A lunatic storm
Threatens, roils, and rumbles
Shattering the calm.

Darkness falls

Wide spread raven's wings,

As black as a moonless lake,

Engulfing the night.

Scars

My scars are beautiful...

Each and every one

Stands as a testament

To proclaim to the world

That the thing that was

Trying to tear me apart

Failed.

Defiant

Stark, desolate wasteland...

A forsaken desert rose

Struggling in solitude;

Life fighting not to die.

Mine

Raking my nails over sleek muscle,

Biting down into rock hard flesh,

I mark my territory.

Alone

Scared

  and scarred

  and alone...

My body

  and heart

  want to cry

But there aren't

  any tears

  left.

Hell

My mind

    is screaming.

My soul

    is bleeding.

It feels

    like dying.

Help me,

    I am in Hell.

Dream fire

Just one more thrill before I die,

Are any of us truly alive?

Self-satisfaction cuts like ice

In this neon concrete paradise.

Lies

We lie to ourselves here.

Maybe we are here

because we lie to ourselves.

Denial, avoidance, rationalization,

Cold-blooded malice,

Perverted justification.

Maybe it will be alright,

Maybe this is where I'm meant to be,

Maybe if I lie enough to myself,

My own lies I will start to believe.

The curse of Eve

To burn for the one who
does not want you,
Every waking moment is torture.
Undesired and discarded,
Life's bitter overture...

Punished for my thoughts,
While forgiven for my deeds.
Lifelong blessings overshadowed—
Dismal curse of Eve.

Broken and ship-wrecked
    in a maelstrom of vices.
Pleading a failing
    of my own devices.

What I crave may not be
what I need.
What I still pray for
the gods do not heed.

A secret forgotten lock...
An ancient fractured key...
I struggle in my understanding
Of why only women have to bleed.

Scream

Strikingly discrepant;

Part injury, part rage

—Call it ferocious

A voice in the dark,

Raw pent-up anger unchained

Will make your world scream.

Ashes

My heart—
a fragrant
night-blooming flower
Is burnt a little bit
blacker
each day.
Drenched in the flames
of an unholy fire,
consumed by Hell.
In the end,
will ashes be
all that remain?

Twisted Venom

I'm fucking adorable,
As cuddly as a razor blade teddy bear,
As sweet as cyanide Koolaid.
A living nightmare
Fueled by anguish and rage.
Vengeance is my specialty,
Overkill is my trademark.
I will peel your skin off
just to watch you bleed,
I will rip your heart out
just to feel it beat.
My hate is visceral,
My fury unstoppable.
You once considered me laughable,
Now welcome to torment unspeakable.

I wanted...

I wanted to send you roses...

but they didn't fit in the envelope.

I wanted to give you a hug...

but it would have wrinkled the paper.

I wanted to send you a kiss...

but the wind blew it away.

I wanted to give you my heart...

but I couldn't find all the pieces.

www.ingramcontent.com/pod-product-compliance
Ingram Content Group UK Ltd.
Pitfield, Milton Keynes, MK11 3LW, UK
UKHW040557210726
13854UKWH00007B/1226

9 781365 589317